Sonny Chua's
Cool Keys
12 irresistible piano solos
1

 For online audio backing tracks played by the composer,
scan the QR code or go to fabermusic.com/audio

Contents

The first waddle 4

Waltz it all about? No.3 5

Dripping fairy 6

Racing against the clock 8

Jive turkey 10

Moonlight whispers 12

Hot diggity 14

Muchocho macho 16

T-Rex hungry 18

Umi's lullaby 20

Tango with my shadow 22

Morning breeze 24

Dedicated to our girls, Aria and Umi

All audio except 'Morning breeze' recorded by Sonny Chua.
'Morning breeze' recorded by Christopher Hussey.

© 2020 by Faber Music Ltd
First published in 2020 by Faber Music Ltd
Bloomsbury House
74–77 Great Russell Street
London WC1B 3DA
Music processed by Jackie Leigh
Cover design by Chloë Alexander
Printed in England by Caligraving Ltd
All rights reserved

ISBN10: 0-571-54183-6
EAN13: 978-0-571-54183-6

To buy Faber Music publications or to find out about the full range of titles available please contact your local retailer or Faber Music sales enquiries:

Faber Music Limited, Burnt Mill, Elizabeth Way, Harlow, CM20 2HX, England
Tel: +44 (0) 1279 82 89 82
fabermusic.com

Celebrating Sonny Chua
(1967–2020)

Sonny Chua was an Australian composer, educator and pianist, known for his characterful and energetic musical style. His music delights in a spirited playfulness and he will undoubtedly be remembered by many for the sheer joy his compositions brought to their playing.

Born in Malaysia, Sonny lived in Kuala Lumpur, Singapore and Malacca before immigrating to Australia. He studied at the Melbourne Conservatorium of Music specialising in piano performance, but his heart was in composing piano music. Sonny composed numerous pieces for his own piano students, taking into account their interests, such as dinosaurs and fairies, but with a pedagogical focus to address various techniques. Sonny was a devoted advocate and spokesperson for music education, resulting in him becoming President of the Association of Music Educators (Victoria). This led to countless workshops, festivals and conferences all over the world, including presenting at the ISME World Conference in Malaysia and Brazil. His piano works are regularly heard at competitions for young musicians and have become standard repertoire in Australian examination syllabuses.

Sonny Chua's Cool Keys 1 and 2 explore a wealth of genres and styles and make for impressive performance pieces. Accompanied throughout by notes from the composer, both books also include audio of all the pieces to download. *Cool Keys 1* was recorded by Sonny himself, providing an invaluable insight into the energy that Sonny's playing exhibits.

We hope these collections of imaginative piano solos will be a fitting tribute to Sonny and inspire pianists of all ages to perform, for many years to come.

The first waddle
The baby duck awakes!

Encourage the duckling to step in time with confident counting in bars 7 and 8, and the last four bars. Make sure the 'quacks' in the right hand are played with personality!

Sonny Chua

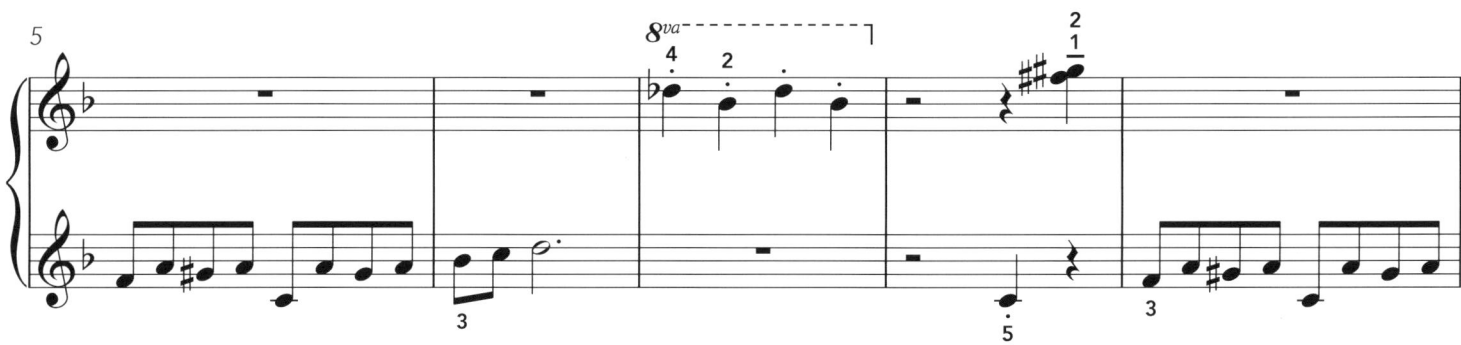

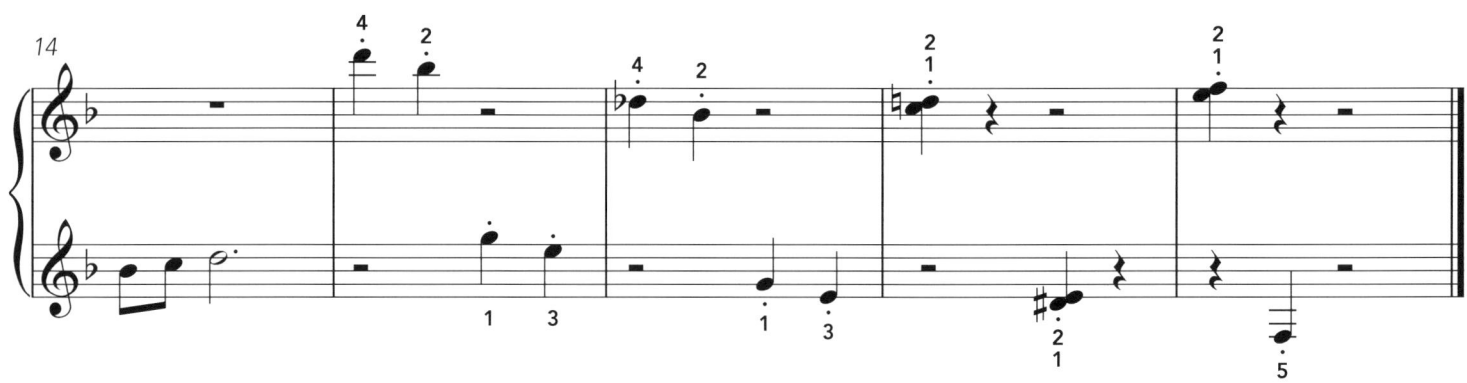

© 2020 by Faber Music Ltd

Waltz it all about? No.3

Capture the bliss of daydreaming with well-shaped phrases. Let the clouds move gently across the clear blue sky with your legato touch as you lay on the grass, breathing with the contour of the melody.

Sonny Chua

Use pedal if you can!

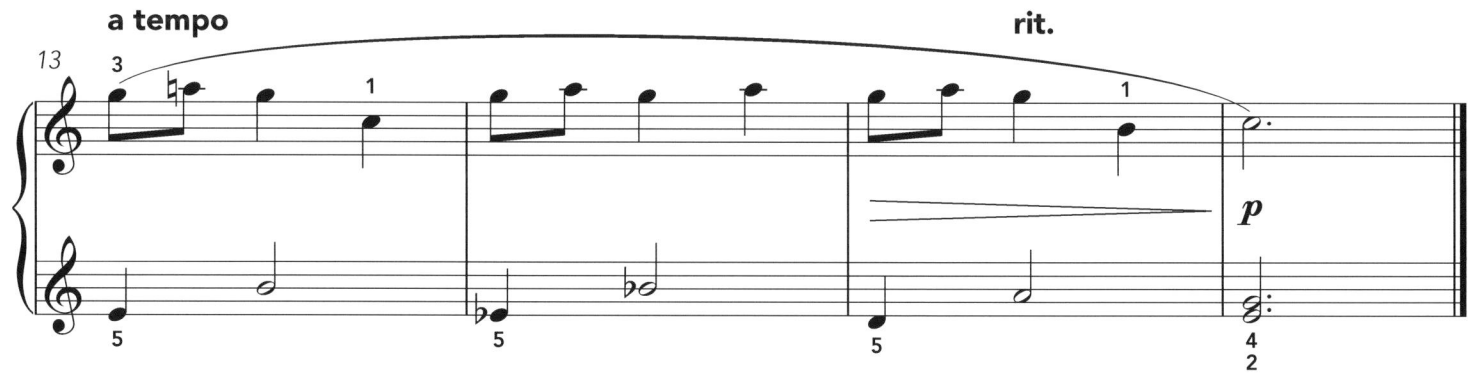

© 2020 Faber Music Ltd

Dripping fairy

Keep the staccato very short and delicate so that it contrasts with the
legato phrases which sound like a slow drip!

Sonny Chua

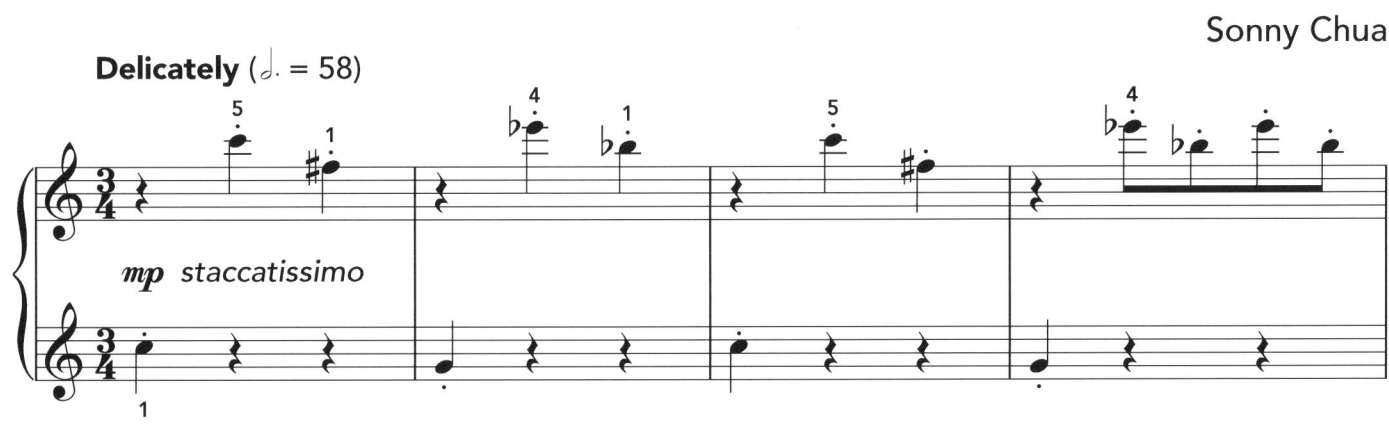
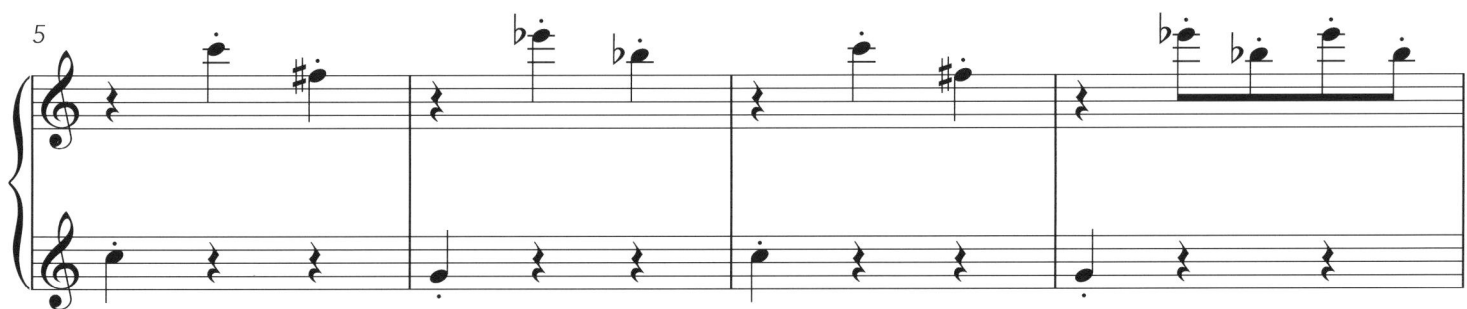
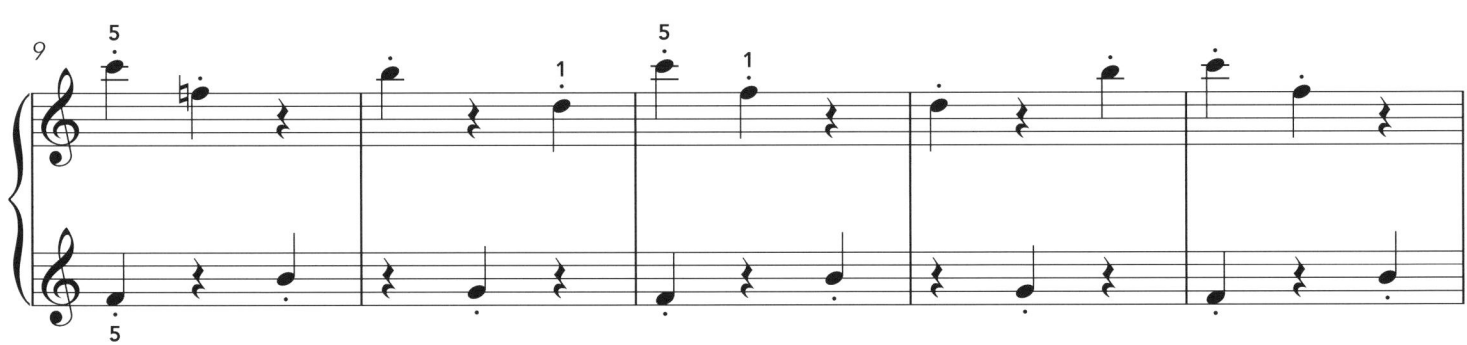
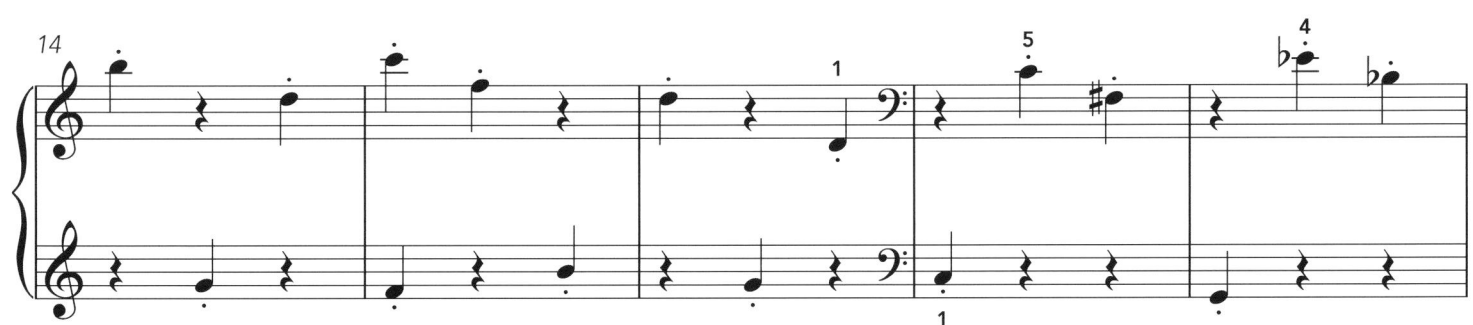

© 2020 Faber Music Ltd

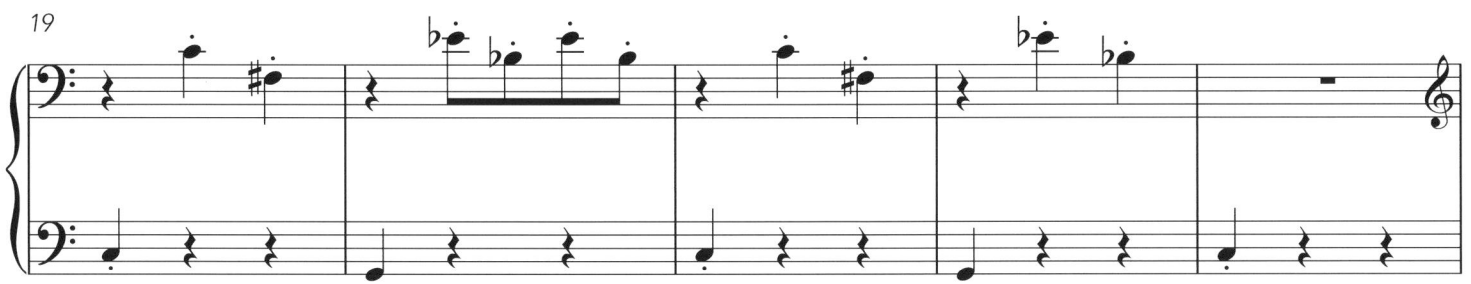
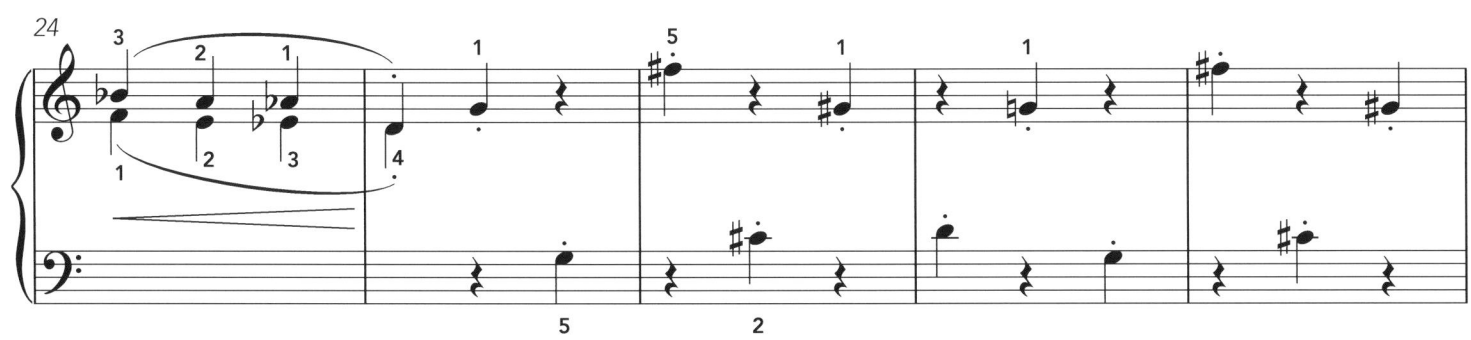
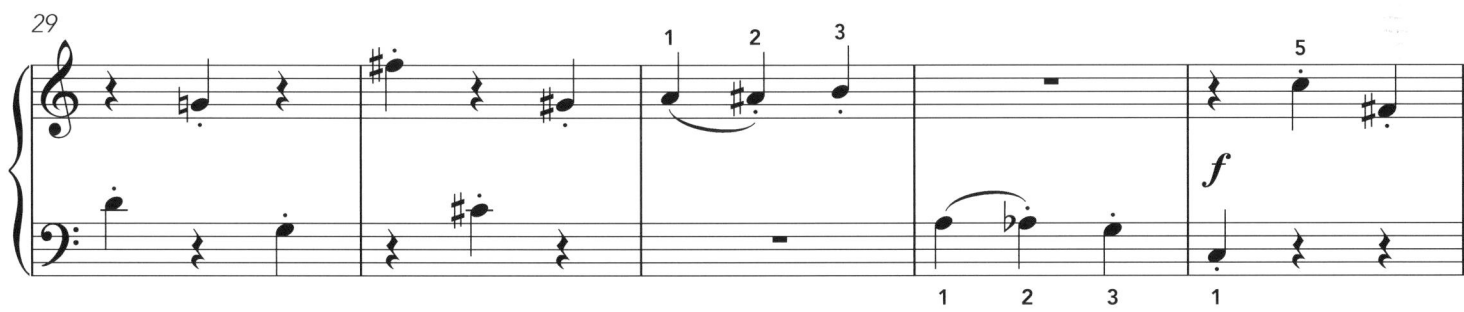

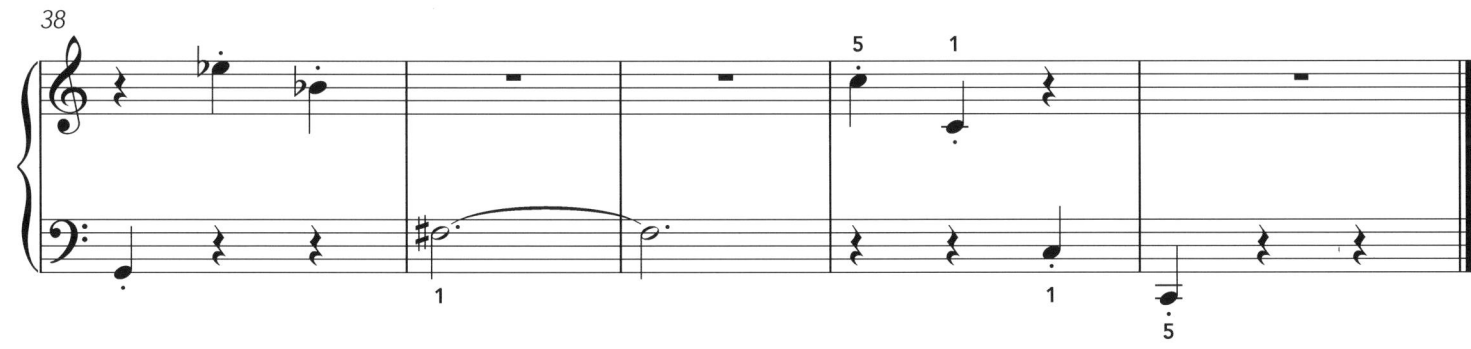

Racing against the clock

This piece should express anxiousness but also a determined energy, just as you would feel in such a situation. Keep the pulse steady to convey the confidence that you will succeed!

Sonny Chua

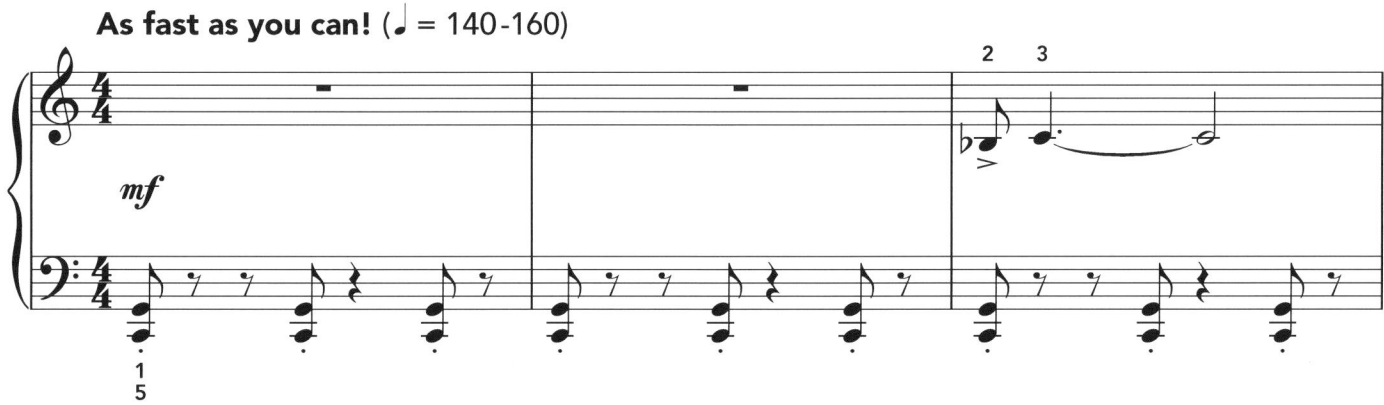

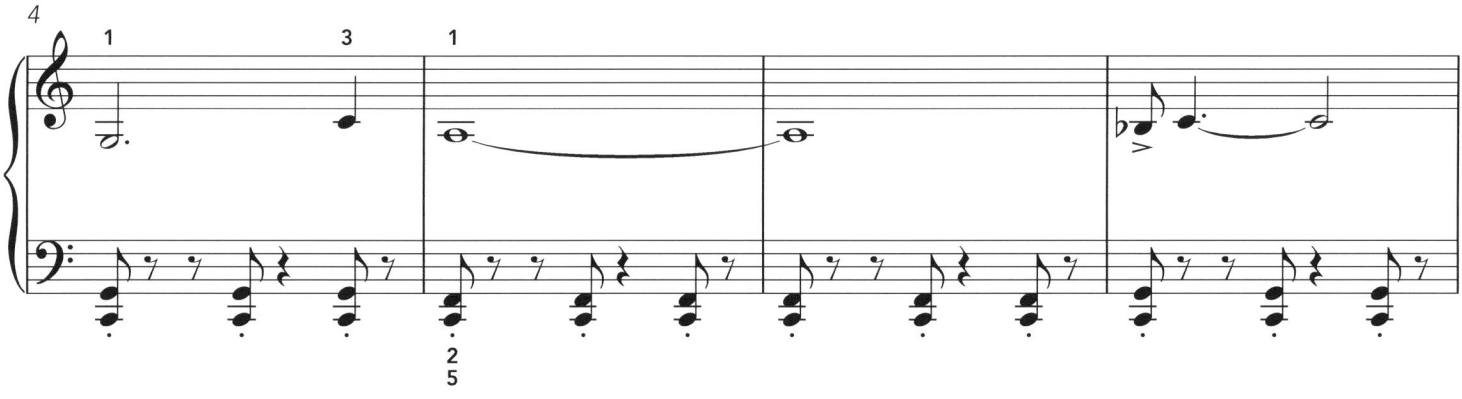

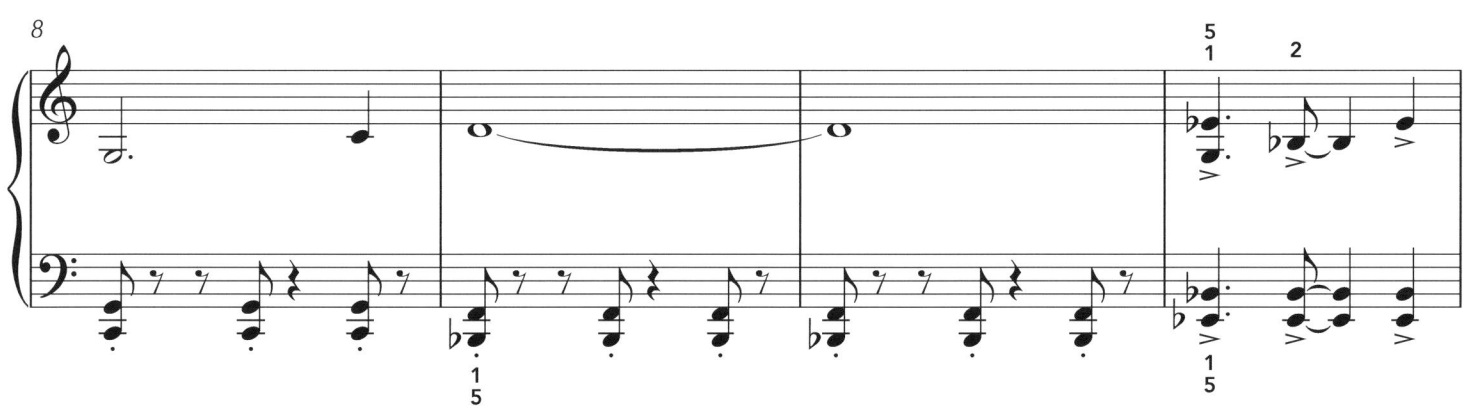

© 2020 Faber Music Ltd

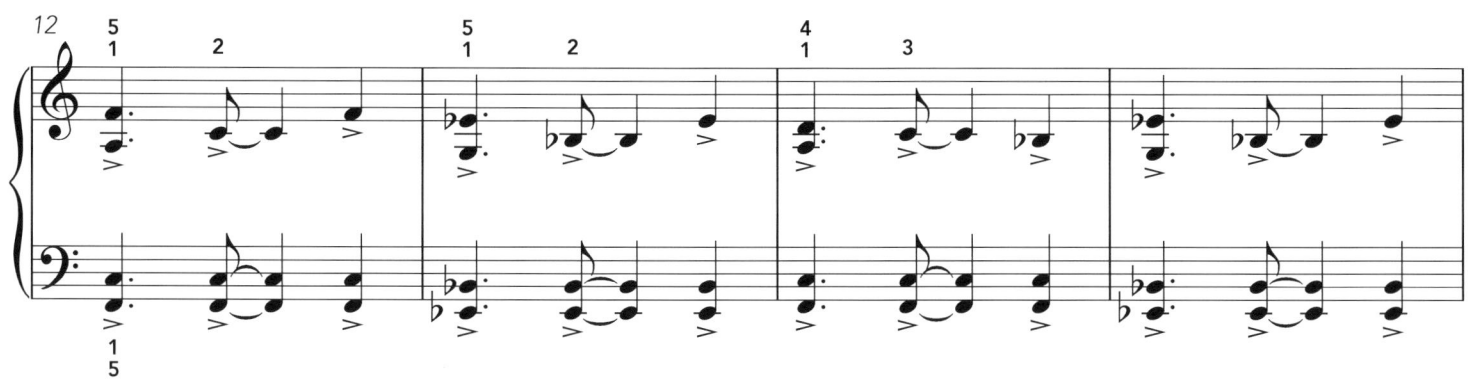

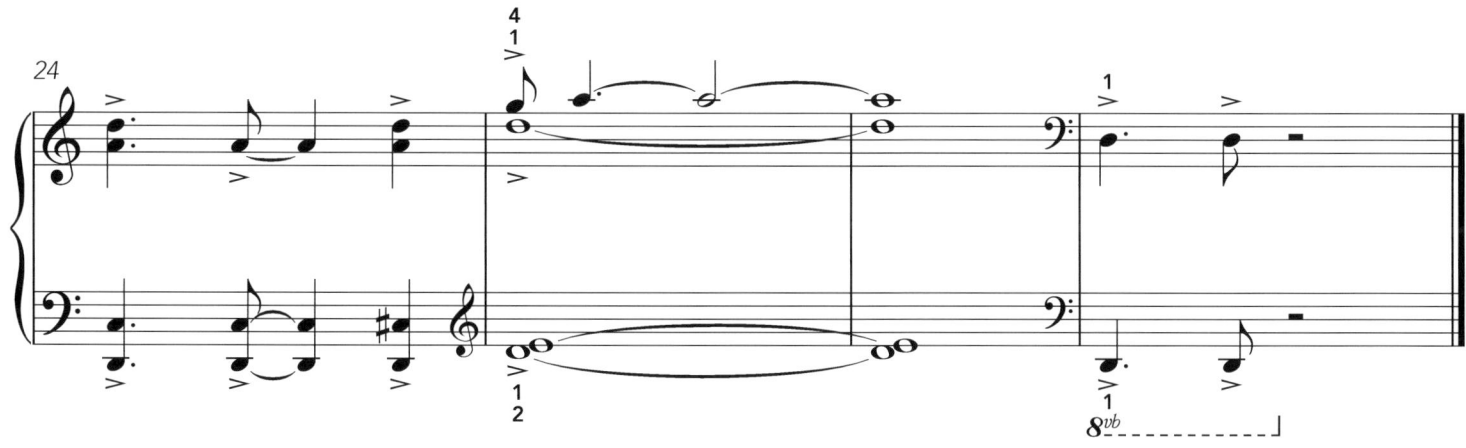

Jive turkey

This is high-octane music that requires you to shake that feather tail!
Keep the pulse steady as you boogie the rhythms.

Sonny Chua

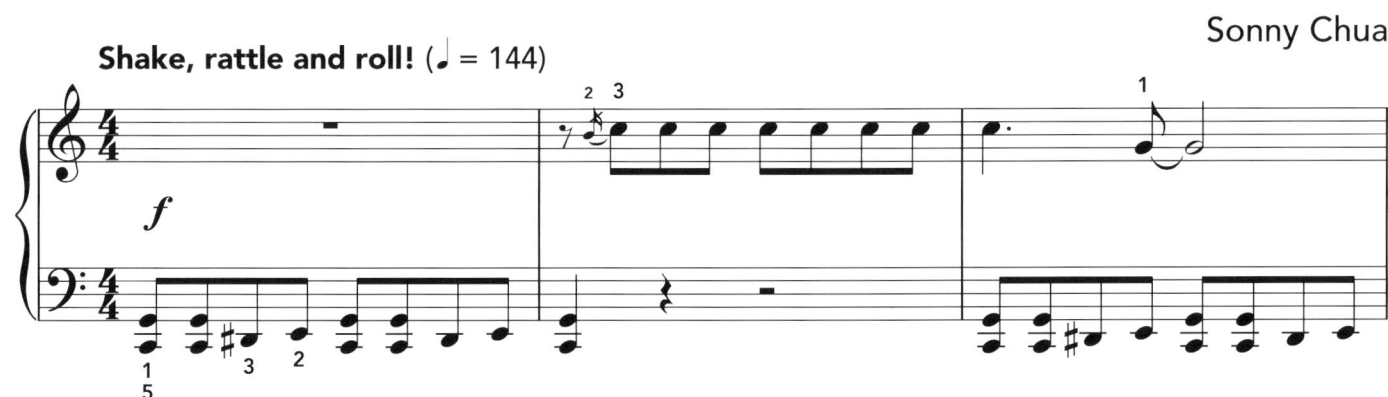

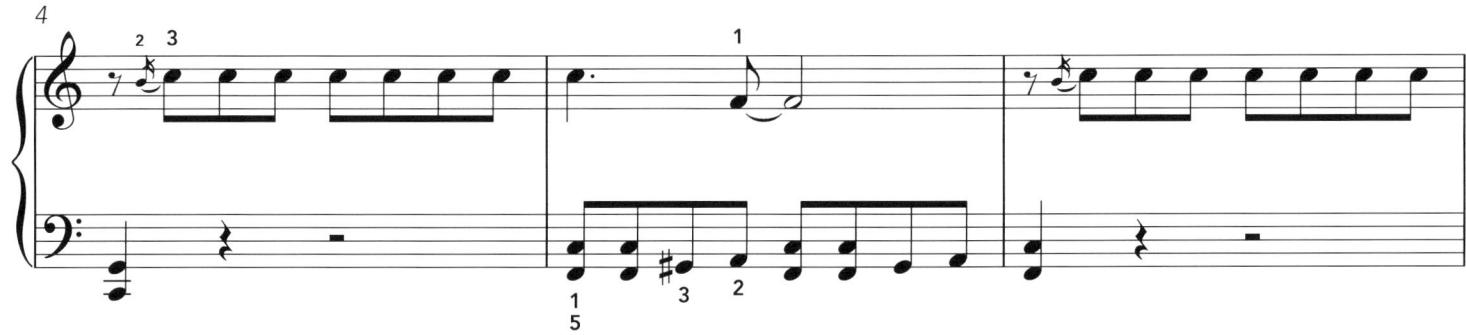

© 2020 Faber Music Ltd

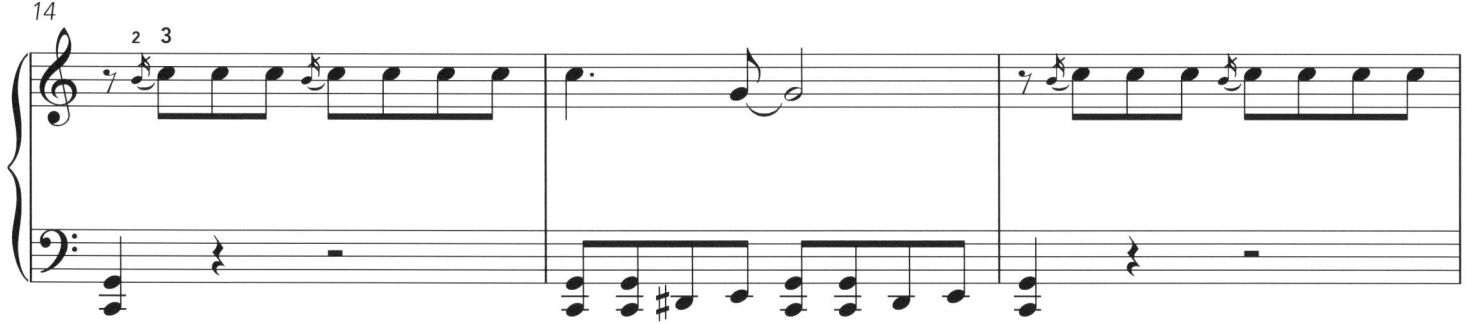

Moonlight whispers

Create a mysterious mood by keeping the phrases smooth and well-shaped.
Allow the sustaining pedal to work its magic, creating mist and tension.

Sonny Chua

© 2020 Faber Music Ltd

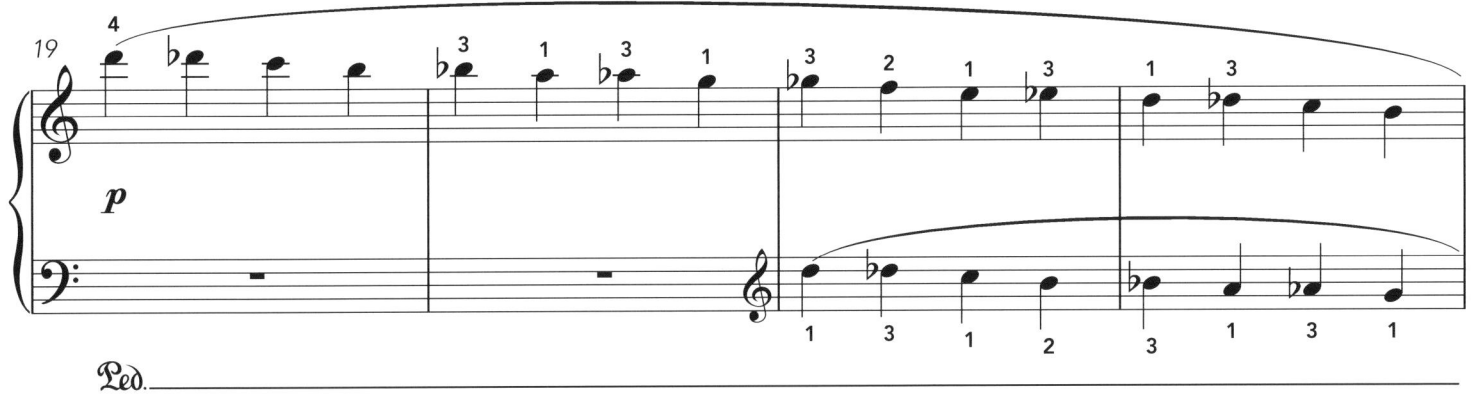

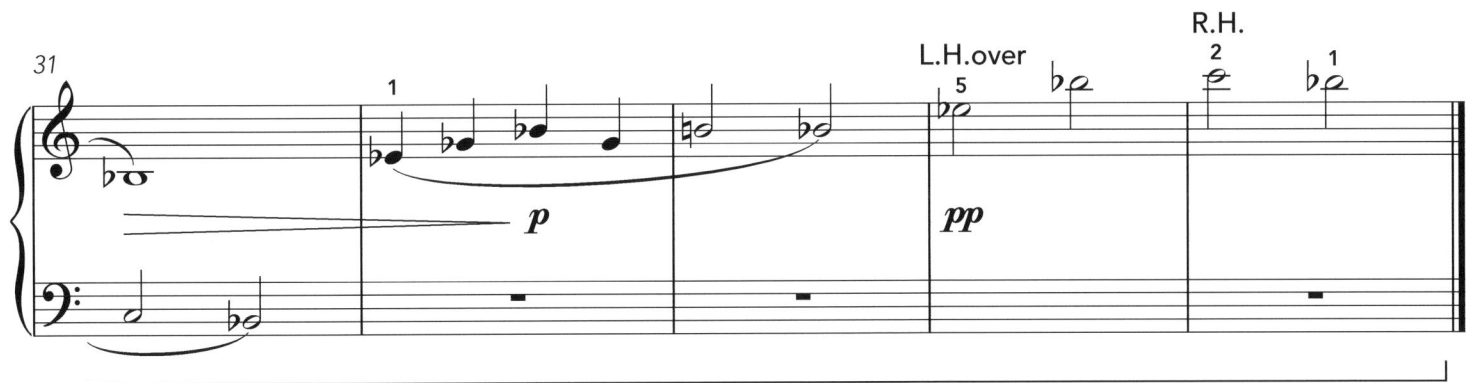

Hot diggity

Taking the time to sort out your fingerings in this piece will really help as it twists and turns.
There are big contrasts in the musical ideas which need the confidence of a super spy at work!

Sonny Chua

© 2020 Faber Music Ltd

Muchocho macho

With dance and rhythmic pieces, it is vital that you feel the pulse strongly and confidently.
Keep the beat ticking away steadily for the time signature changes,
like remaining balanced on a horse as it changes direction.

Sonny Chua

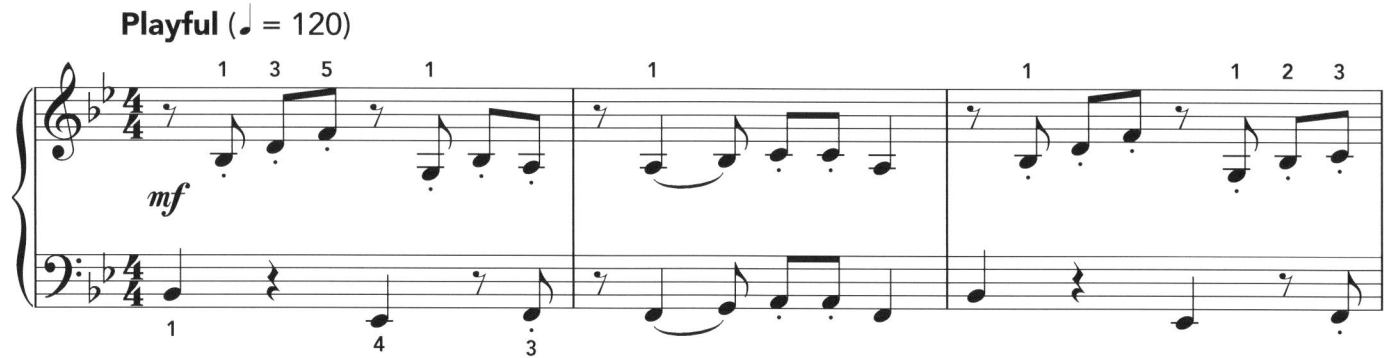

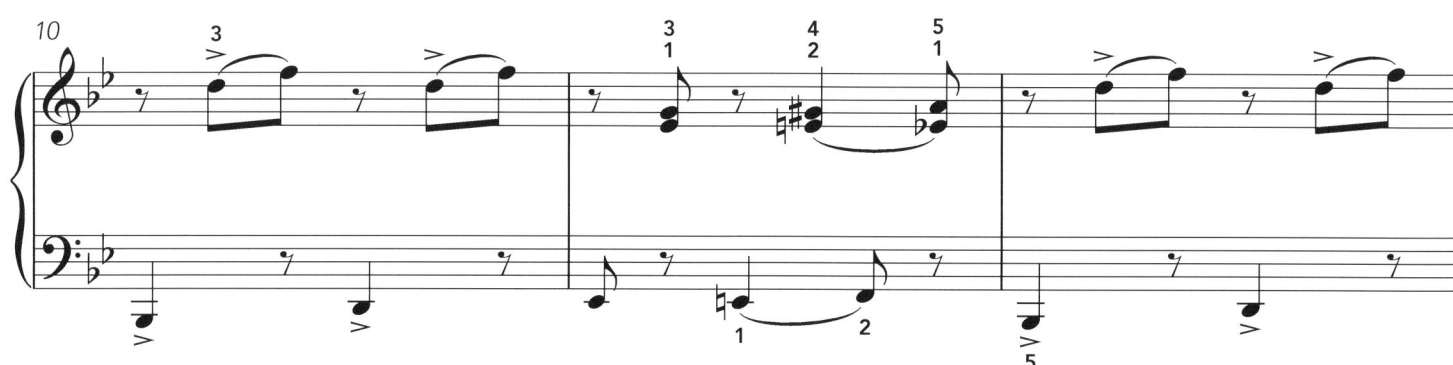

© 2020 Faber Music Ltd

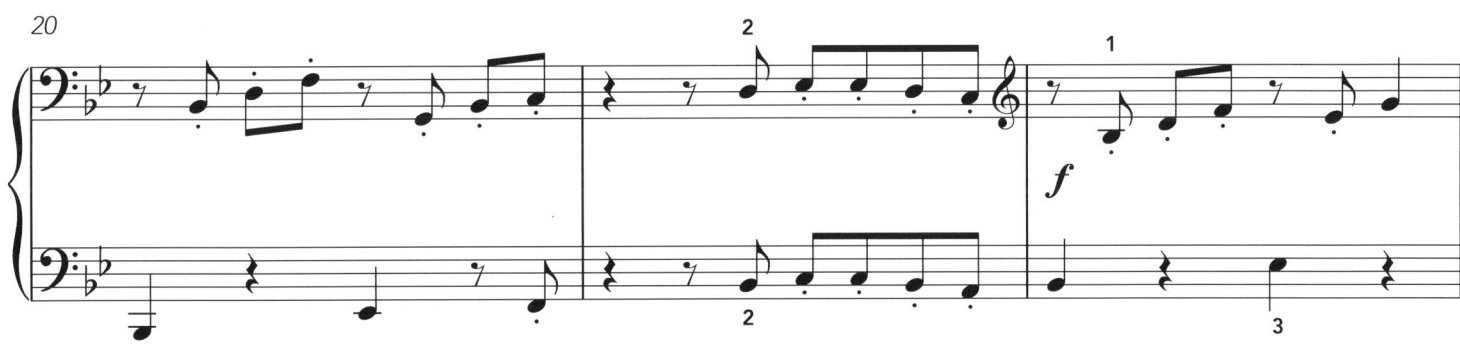

Mu - cho - cho ma - cho!

T-Rex hungry

Attack the accents ferociously! This T-Rex takes no prisoners. This is
aggressive and angry music which requires a strong handle on the pulse.
Make the contrast of dynamics extreme! But save your loudest snap for the end.

Sonny Chua

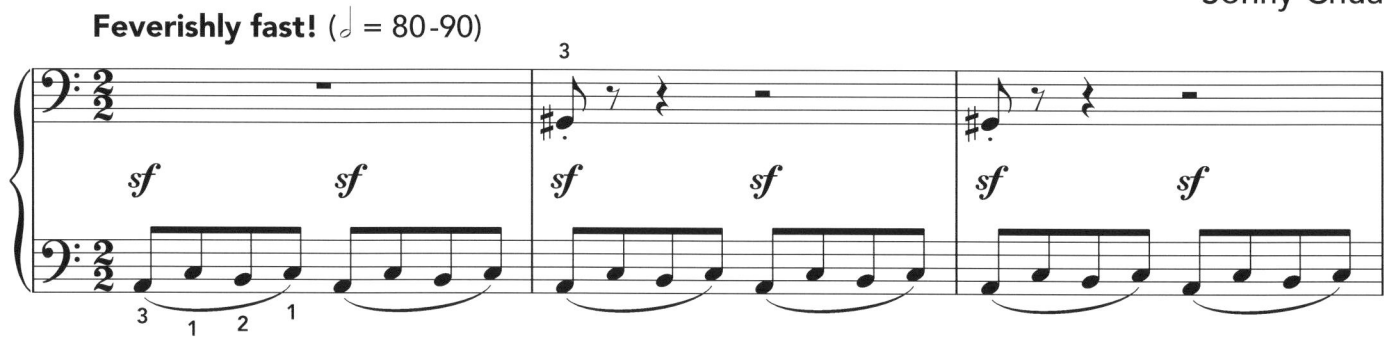

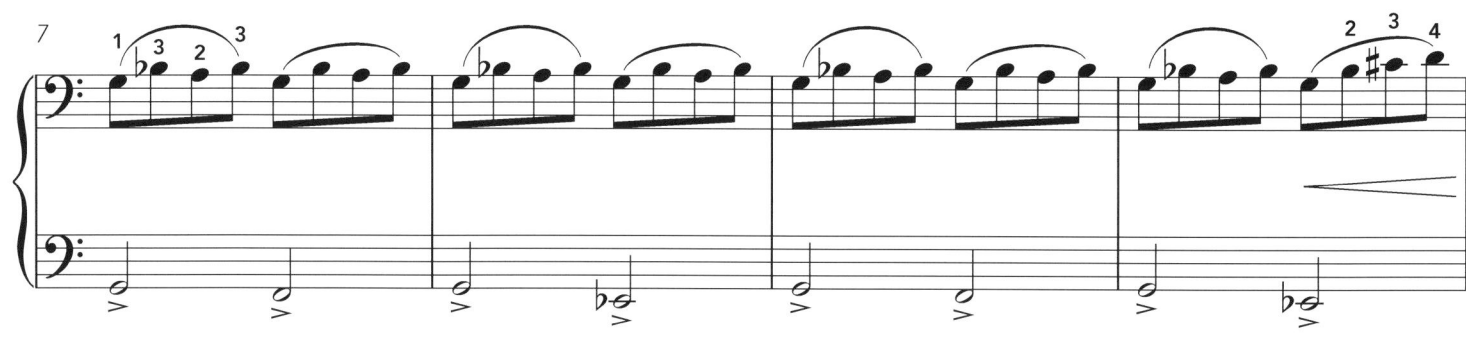

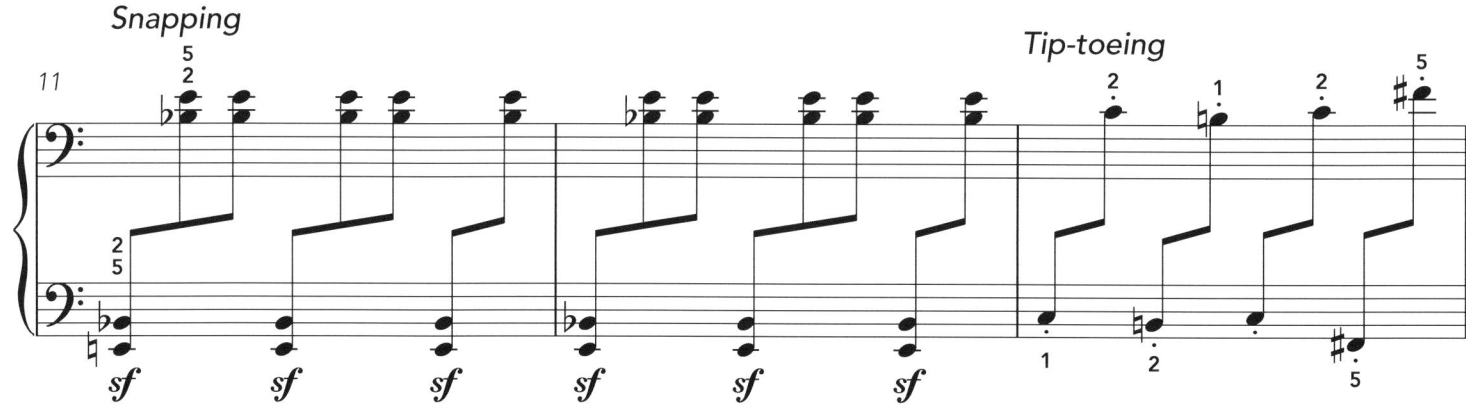

© 2020 Faber Music Ltd

Umi's lullaby

This piece was written about my first child just before she came into the world and is meant to convey overwhelming love and awe. As it is a lullaby, play delicately but make sure you look at the fingerings carefully so you can hold the baby securely in your hands.

Sonny Chua

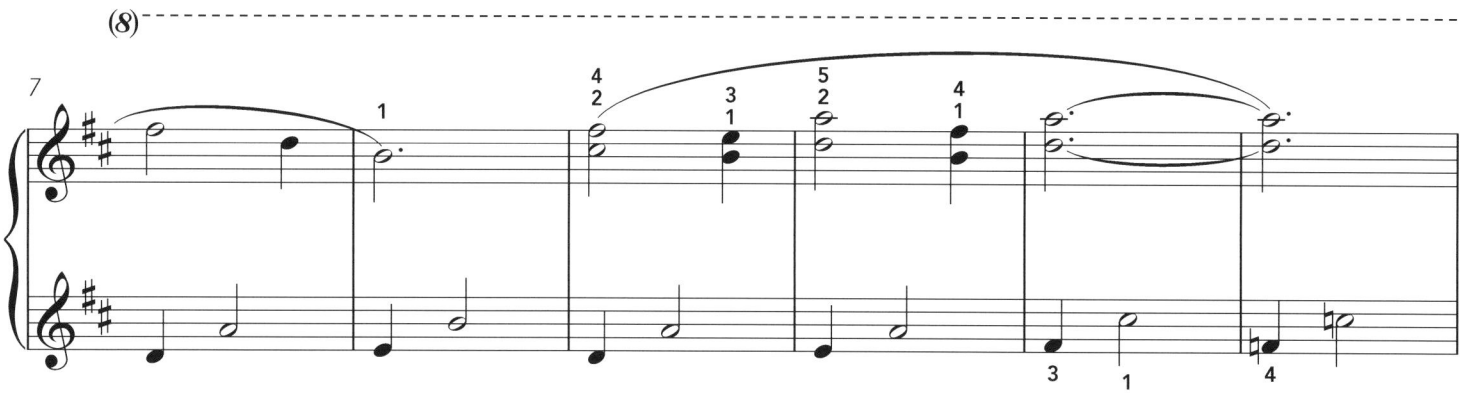

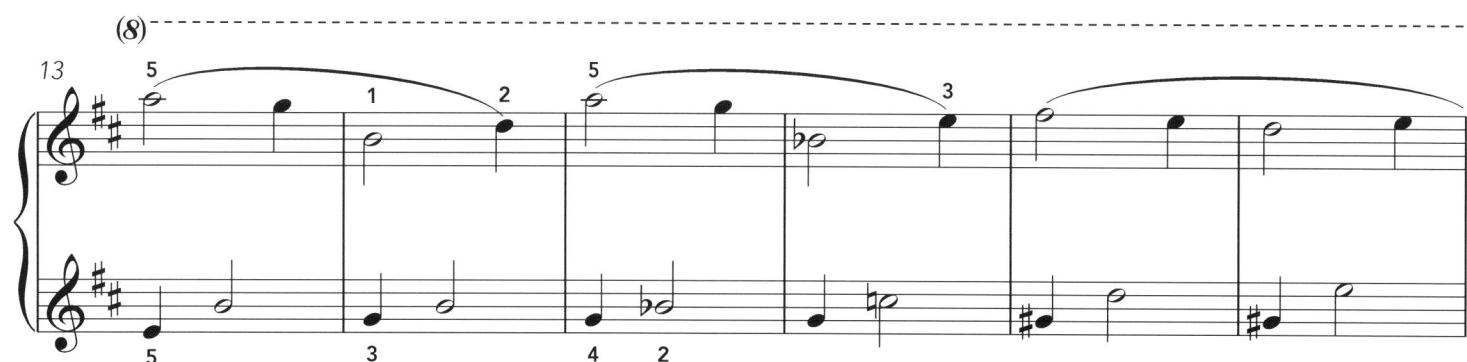

© 2020 Faber Music Ltd

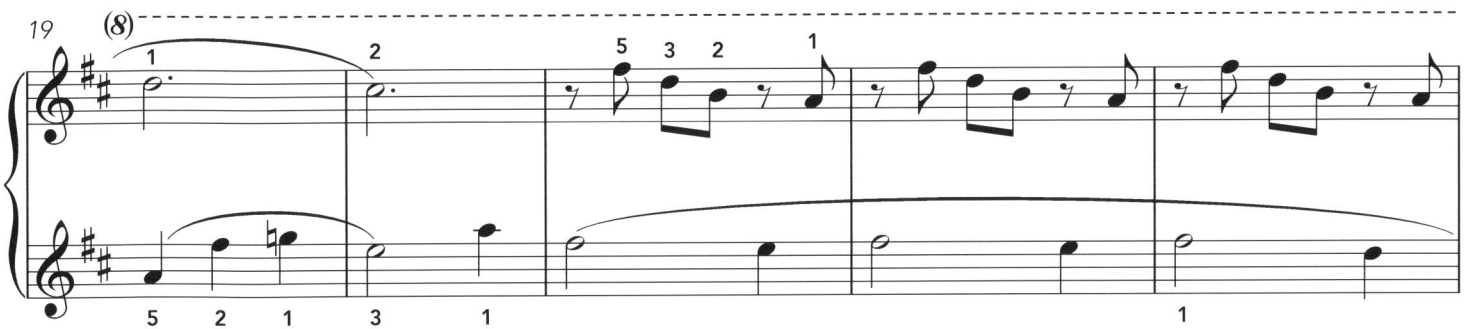
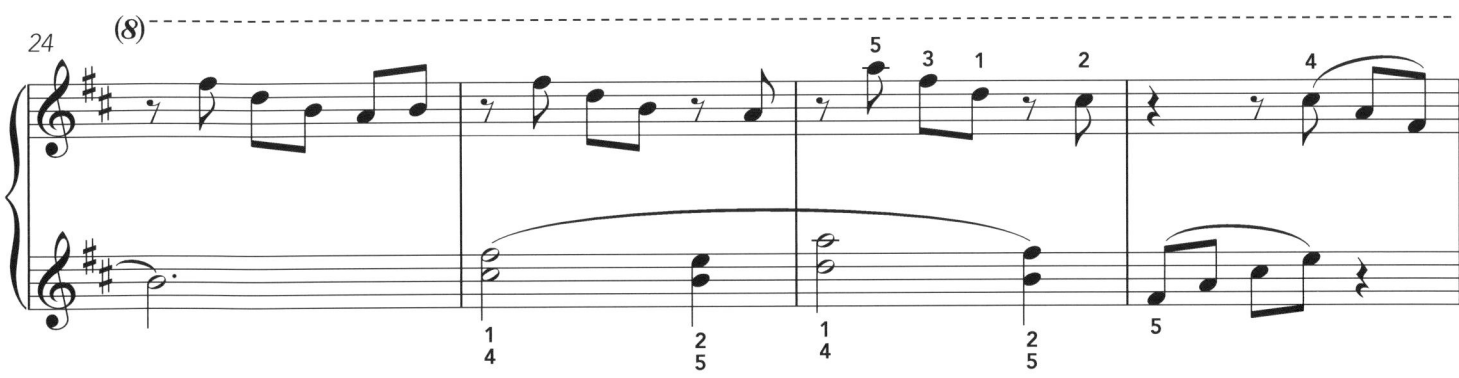
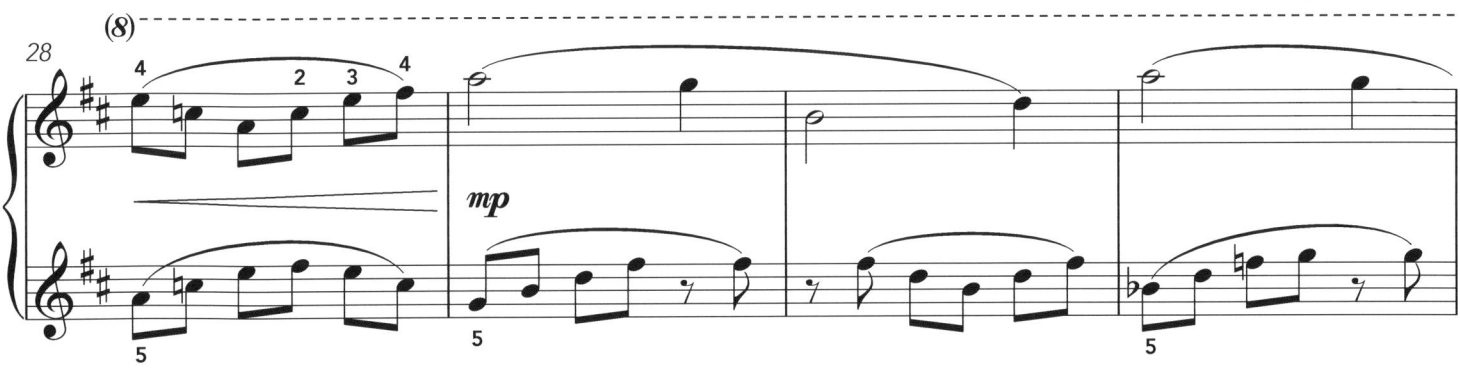
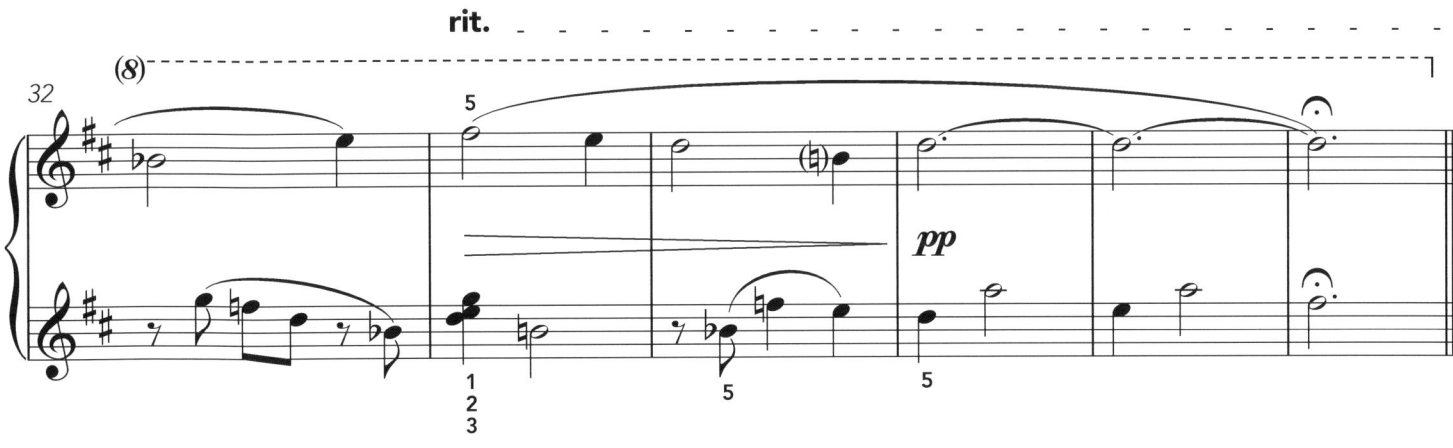

Tango with my shadow

The shadow is a tricky thing and the tango is a cheeky a dance! Keep the pulse steady
and be sure to surprise everyone with the passion of the sharp accents,
a contrast to the swooping cantabile phrases.

Sonny Chua

*click/clap/stomp!

© 2020 Faber Music Ltd

Morning breeze

Sonny Chua